I Will Always Love You, Ella

By Kris Patterson

TABLE OF CONTENTS

DEDICATION

I dedicate this book to the memory and spirit of Colleen Deederly. Her unceasing efforts to help people with their grief and being there to listen were my inspiration for this book. I know she was happy with the idea and I am sorry she didn't get to see the finished product but the funds will go to ensuring her work continues.

Colleen was able to take a personal tragedy and create something positive and help other people. I dedicate this book to the spirit and memory of this incredible person.

A precious, sweet little girl, Ella
Whose stay was not long enough,
Yet touched so many,
Gone to heaven above,
Oh, how we'll miss you baby, Ella Rose
Leaving us memories,
Never to be forgotten,
Forever in our thoughts and our hearts.
A precious baby now, and
An angel above who we dearly love,
God bless you precious baby girl...Ella Rose Freya Patterson

By Skylar and Tara Patterson

FOREWORD

I spoke with Colleen Deederly on Tuesday August 21, 2012 about my desire to raise some funds for the compassionate friends and I realized I was on the right path. I also realized how much talking to someone who understands can help. I felt like I was crazy for a lot of the rage and hurt I was feeling, but it is reassuring to know I was not alone. I hope this will translate to my book as well. It is important to feel that you are normal when your world is spinning out of control. Colleen mentioned how important the butterfly was to her as a symbol due to the transitional nature of life. We also shared a common view that whatever form of healing you do is good as long as you get it out. When you don't cry and let it out it will destroy you. I have definitely held onto mine for too long.

Colleen totally understood me and it was nice to get some of it out even years later. She had talked about a lady who was at Fir Park Village and said she had lost her child 50 years ago and it was always there. Lately I have thought I was getting better but a lot of the things are coming back. I was hoping the book will help me as well with that. I have had to re-examine everything including reliving and dwelling on those difficult memories. I don't know if that is the best way to write the book but I need to process it in this way.

Colleen and I spoke at length about the Compassionate Friends Association. We talked a lot about our mutual experiences which although are different have many of the same feelings and emotions. She said a lot of the people think that because it has been years they don't feel like they need the meetings anymore. I don't know if it ever goes away and I want to support the organization any way I can. I want it to be there for anyone who needs it and I hope that this book will play a part in making that happen. I feel like I should have met with Colleen years ago, now that I know the kind of person she is and how healing sharing can be now that I have felt it first hand. I noticed she said that her sorrow led her to the Compassionate Friends and how people have told her how much it has helped other people and her sorrow helped her fill a void in this community so something positive has come from her experience. I would like to thank Colleen for her time with me and for her service to Port Alberni. Colleen passed away suddenly on September 9, 2012. I know that she has inspired me and others with her example of how to live and I will never forget the compassion that Colleen has shown me.

Look to this day
For it is life
The very life of life.

In its brief course lie all
The realities and truths of existence
The joy of growth
The splendor of action
The glory of power.

For yesterday is but a memory
And tomorrow is only a vision.
But today well lived
Makes every yesterday a memory
Of happiness
And every tomorrow a vision of hope.

Look well, therefore, to this day....

~ Ancient Sanskrit poem ~

INTRODUCTION

Although eight years have passed, I was not able to write this book before because some of the emotions were much too raw to be expressed. Even eight years later going through this process has been heart wrenching for me. I think it might have been worse because some of these undealt with memories have gathered momentum and power throughout the years. I do hope Ella will be proud of this book.

The time has come for me to open myself up and allow my hurt to help others. It has taken me this long to be able to speak about it. It is a good time to memorialize Ella and ensure she will be remembered for the important piece of my life that she is.

As long as people understand that it is okay to ask for help and gather a little strength from my story then it is all worth it. This book will be part biography of Ella's short but important life as well as some of my insights and experiences going through this tumultuous time.

I had been holding onto a lot of feelings and not sure how to express them in regards to Ella for many years. I realized that I had to do something constructive with them or they would eat me up. I spent many years wallowing in self pity and pain. For some reason now seems like the right time to complete this book. I had originally written several pages about her life and some of the experiences that came from it. I actually did that for myself because I was afraid I would forget her. I am glad I did write those pages as they formed the nucleus of the book I am writing now. It was hard to relive a lot of those times but I felt it was necessary to honestly express myself and my feelings in this book. I have always tried to help people and now I think this is an opportunity to help others and myself. I have always felt that Ella deserved to be remembered. After talking with Colleen Deederly I realized how there are people out there who understand. I used to feel like I was crazy for some of the thoughts I had. I wavered many times when writing this book as I thought it was wrong to talk about your feelings. I realize that it is healing to let out some of the pain and that there are people, good people out there who understand and who care. Colleen was able to effect a positive change through her tragedy and I hope to be able to contribute something to an incredible organization. I dedicate this book to everyone who has ever lost someone particularly a child. It is a cruel world that has a parent burying a child. It is completely backwards to the way the world is supposed to operate. Nothing can steal peace and joy and undermine the very foundation of someone's life like losing a child. It is devastating on a level that most of us can't imagine. I hope that this book reaches the person that needs it at the moment they need it most and it offers some hope.

The death of a child is like no other loss. Although Ella was with us for only a short period of time, the lessons she taught me were profound, so profound in fact it took me years to understand some of them and to put them into practice. I am not sure I have fully learned them. I have always wanted to honor her and her memory. She was a piece of my life and a piece of my heart. I have always prided myself on being tough and pretending things didn't bother me, but that is a lie. There is no feeling on this earth of sitting helpless while a child, that you helped create lay dying and there is absolutely nothing you can do, no amount of begging, pleading or bargaining can change that outcome. I hope that no person ever has to feel that feeling again.

It is with great trepidation that I write this book and have it published because it shows me in a light of vulnerability which I never wanted to portray and maybe never wanted to believe I had in the first place. But part of this book is about closure and in order to get closure it requires honesty with me and my feelings. Showing vulnerability is a part of the growth I have been working on. This requires a completely different perspective from what I've always been used to. I always pretended I was okay and never needed help. The purpose of this book is not to make people cry although it is okay if it does make you cry because that is an emotional response to grief we all have.

Everybody understands grief and loss, perhaps not the loss of a child. This book will also expose me for my true self and up to recently I was never proud of that person, because there were things I could have done better. The situation and how I handled it, or more importantly didn't handle it are some of the most colossal failures I have experienced in my life. The fact that I have been unable to rectify that has always sat poorly with me. I recently had the great pleasure of creating another book which increased my skills and confidence to think I could finally complete this project. The time is now to move forward to finish this book for my own self and my healing. I have a lot of stuff inside to get out. I do hope that the pain I have felt and experienced will help at least one other person. I have always prided myself on someone who cares about others. Every experience you have makes you who you are today. I will always love Ella and for years I shut down my feelings toward her and everything else which was the wrong direction to go. I want to become the person that Ella would have been proud of. The time has come for me to accept everything that has happened and move beyond it.

To see someone I helped bring into this world die had a profound affect on my life and my thoughts for the future. I think the sorrow of losing Ella changed me into a different person, it later focused me, my sorrow has allowed me to see and do things which I never believed myself capable of. A lot of the ideas have been floating around but they now are beginning to take shape. It's like the sorrow brought out some potential there that may not have been realized without it.

Ella's life taught me to appreciate life, all life. It was a lesson that took me a long time to learn. I drifted through life with no goals or ambitions. This lifestyle became a comfortable habit which I allowed myself to wallow in for several years. The loss of my parents later reinforced this lesson. I needed to learn about respecting life including my own and I was afraid to ask for help or even admit that I needed help. I hid behind a facade of false optimism and a cloak of fake humor. It was important to me that people thought I was strong. I took a stubborn tack on this and I know now that it severely held back my healing.

"Love is like water which flows in our veins freely. It can satisfy us relieve our thirst and sustain us, for it's a life giver. But when it is blocked, it's an ache which surpasses all other physical ailments. It will bang against that blockage until eventually that love will leak away like water down a sink. Then we will no longer live, do that life giver is gone and we are nothing more than a hollow shell."

Thursday February 5, 2004

Ella Rose Freya Patterson is born at 10:27am. She was 7 pounds 5.5 ounces. We chose the name Ella after Patty's Grandfather Archie Thompson's mother Ella. I originally thought it was an old fashioned name, but the more I thought about it I liked it. I remember going to Archie to ask his permission and see what he thought. He was honored.

This was the happiest day of my life. I was so proud of Ella and I remember my mom telling me how she was the best anniversary gift ever. It was a difficult delivery and I was very happy. When Ella was born she slid across my hand and gave me an electric shock.

I spent the morning playing the role of the proud father. I had

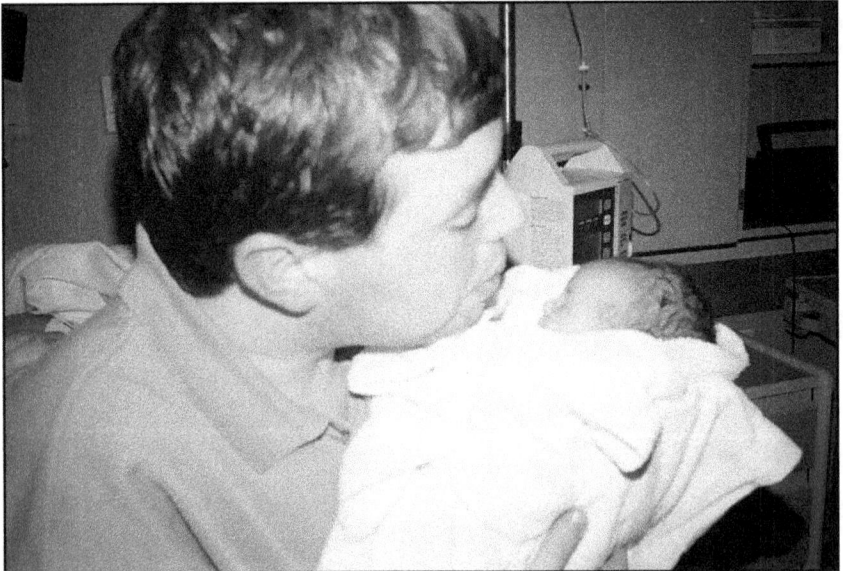

My first proud moment as a new father

everybody posing for photos. I am very glad I did. Those photos became very precious to me.

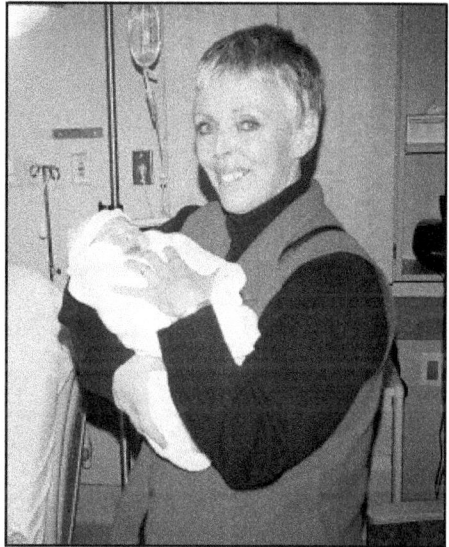

My Mom overjoyed with her grand daughter. I don't think anyone held her more.

Don't cry for me Daddy,
I'm right here.
Although you can't see me
I see your tears.
I visit you often,
I go to work with you each day,
And when it's time for you
To close your eyes,
On your pillow is where I lay.
I hold your hand &
Stroke your hair,
And whisper in your ear.
If you're sad today Daddy,
Remember, I am here.
God took me home.
This we know is true.
But you'll always be My Daddy
Even though I'm not with you.
We will never be apart,
For every time you think of me,
Please know I'm in your Heart..........

~Author Unknown

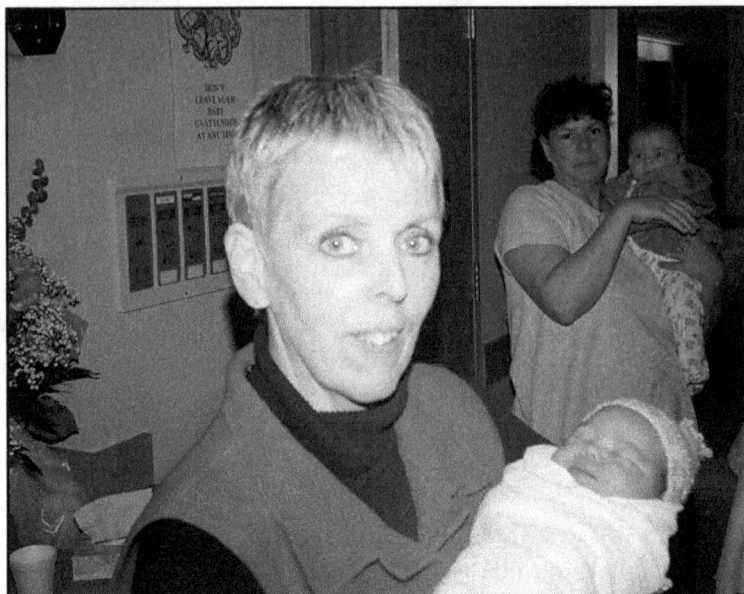

Another photo with my mom and Ella.

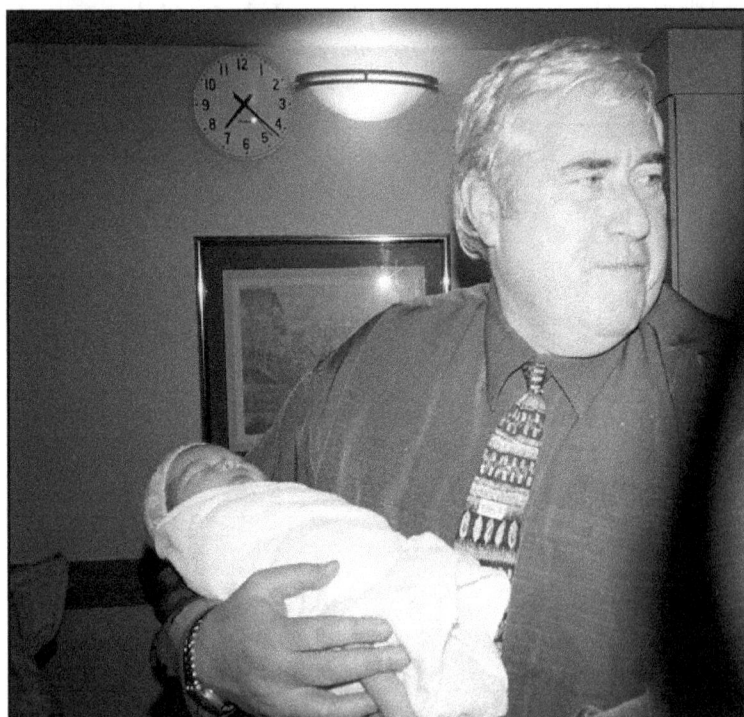

Proud Grandpa posing for a photo

Friday February 6, 2004

Ella stopped feeding from the breast at 3pm. She had some jaundice which required her to go under lights. At 9pm she stopped feeding all together and threw up bile. I went to go home to get the house ready to bring everyone home. I received a call that I needed to come back to the hospital as there was a problem. I always regretted leaving to get things ready. If I would have known what was going to happen, I would have spent every spare second with her. The hospital here didn't know what the problem was and later a team was called in from Vancouver. I have always placed my faith in people greater than myself. I felt like Children's Hospital was the best and they would find the problem and fix it.

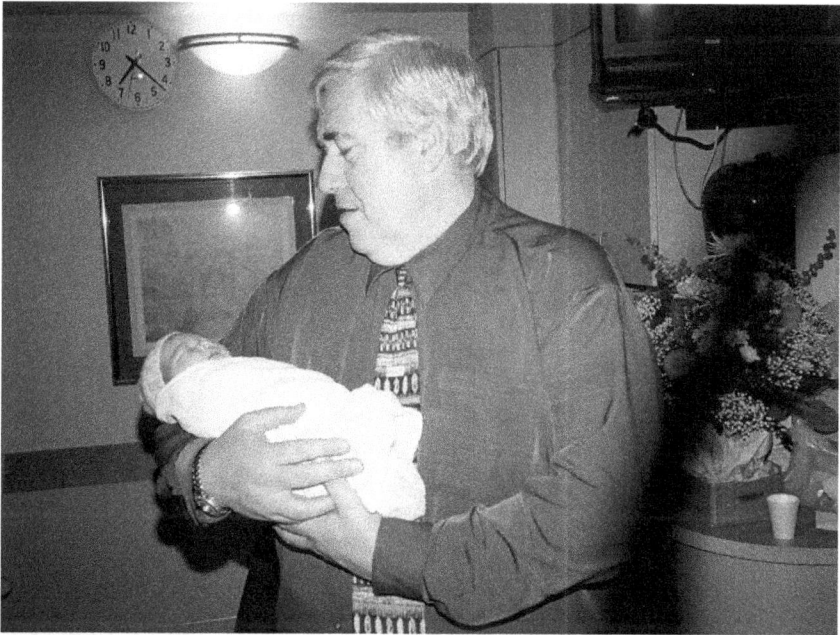

My dad with Ella. I remember Ike telling me how proud he was of me.

7

Saturday February 7, 2004

Ella continued to worsen today. Dr. McCollister returned from a conference in Victoria to see her. He suggested that she be flown to Vancouver to Children's Hospital. Patty and I drove with mom down on the 3pm ferry. When we got there she had a tube to drain the bile and she had stabilized. A hospital has never been my favorite place, especially in these circumstances. When I got there I talked to her and she squeezed my finger and turned to me. Patty said whenever I spoke Ella would always try to get closer to the sound of my voice. I did spend many nights talking to Ella before she was born, telling her of my plans and dreams and all of things that she was going to be able to see and do. She seemed to be doing better. They ran many tests including one where dye is circulated through your system. At 11:10 Dr. Chessex asked for my consent for surgery, they found she had a perforated bowel and this had gone into her system and gone septic. I was devastated but I felt that at least we had now discovered the problem and now that we knew what it is, we could fix it.

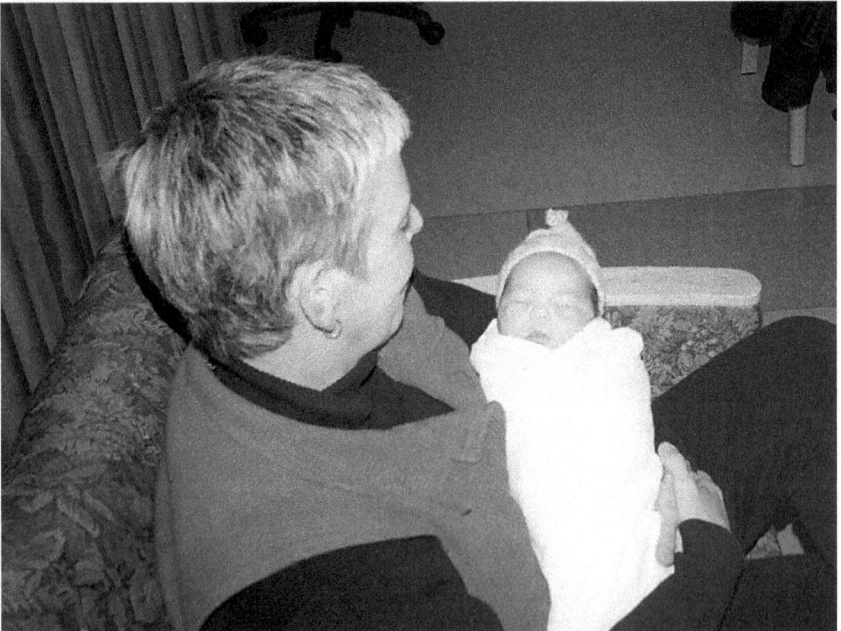

Ella always responded to my mom. She was so at ease in my mom's arms.

The Dark Place

I was there again today,
To the Dark Place,
Deep Below the Surface
Where Light cannot reach
I do not choose to go there
It comes to find me
Drags me with hidden claws
Into its Chasm of sadness

Sunday February 8, 2004

I remember seeing Ella when I returned to the hospital. We had been told she was on life support and there was not much hope with the situation and eventually she would shut down completely. I have never been an overly religious man, however I prayed like I have never prayed before. I also bargained. I was willing to give up my life if it meant she would recover. I concentrated so hard on this that I felt like something broke inside me.

My mom drove us down to Vancouver and left on the last ferry back to Port Alberni. I was 28 years old at this time and I still wanted my mom to stay. The way things progressed she ended up coming back on the first ferry the next morning with my dad.

At 2am Dr. Chessex said the operation was finished and he had to do an oleoscopy which means that a portion of her intestine was left out of her body and would require an ostomy bag for a while. Dr. Chessex let us know at 2am the results of the surgery. At 6:30 Dr. Chessex let us know about an infection and complications.

7am began the longest day of my life. I could do nothing but watch and wait helplessly. I tried willing her to get better and I knew she had my strength and I had hoped that sheer will would allow her to recuperate. The doctors tried everything humanly possible. Eventually the machines were doing more and more of the work for her system. Dr. Chessex took us in the back room and explained about how if she recovered from this set back, that the doctors had to remove so much of her intestines that there was a real concern if she would be able to process food. We pretty much just held on to her and talked to her. The cardiologist said her heart was beating wrong and too hard. We were told it was only a matter of time and that there was no hope. The acidity of her blood which should be at zero was climbing every time they took samples, despite everything they were doing. Dr. Chessex said he couldn't guarantee that Ella was not suffering. A family meeting was held during which the decision to remove her from life support had to be made. That was the hardest decision I have ever had to make in my life and one that I grapple with to this day. My dad, who was always the strongest person I have ever known broke down, got up and had to leave the room,. This was the first time I remember seeing my father cry. I felt like I let so many people down including Ella.

We decided to stop all treatment and let her pass peacefully. We asked to hold her one last time without the tubes. They took her off the machines at 4:00. At 4:08 Ella Rose Freya Patterson took her last breath in my arms. The sound of this continues to haunt me. To this day I felt like I should have let her mother hold her for this, I was not strong enough. I also remember telling her not to cry because I didn't want Ella's last memory to be us crying over her. She left this world at 4:08pm on February 8, 2004. My watch also stopped at 4:08.

It is funny the memories that you hold onto and how quickly the sound of something will take you right back to that moment. One of those was leaving the hospital and the sound of those automatic doors opening and we were leaving with no child, I didn't know how to feel, I was numb and empty. I remember my dad telling my mom maybe she should drive and I don't remember anything else except going below the deck on the ferry. I hesitate to tell this part of the story because it shows me at my weakest moment. The best way I can explain this is by saying I was empty and the only thing I had was this aching emptiness and the moment was too much for me. I didn't see an end to the pain I was in. I had climbed over the metal grate and I was looking down at the water which was black and very choppy. The wind was very strong. My worst nightmare was seeing her alone in the darkness, scared and alone, with no one to help her. As I went to jump something shiny caught my eye and broke my mindset and I looked down and it was a tiny angel figure with a stone. Looking at this figure made me

The Angel pin that I found on the Ferry

think about what I was about to do and how that would hurt the people I cared about most. I climbed back over the railing and returned to my family on the upper deck, never mentioning my moment of weakness to anybody.

I was working at Dob City bingo hall at the time and everyone was waiting to hear about how everything turned out as Ella was overdue and the customers were all waiting for the good news. I couldn't face the people and have to explain the story over and over again. I had my mom phone in and let Norma know what had happened and I took two weeks off to try and get some things figured out. There was so much to do as the apartment was set up with cribs and baby stuff. I wanted to be alone to climb into myself as soon as we got home. I was unable to do this as there were so many people there. I look back on this time and realize it was good for Ella's mom to have her traditional culture from which to draw strength. I felt like an outsider during this time as I didn't know what was to happen and it seemed like my part of her was coming second to everything else. My best friend Wayne White was there for me. I had begun to drink heavily as an escape and I remember the day Wayne told me that it was enough that it was not what Ella would have wanted. I needed to hear that and a good friend is someone who will tell you what you need to hear whether you want to hear it or not.

I wrote a few pages about Ella originally for myself and because even though Ella was only with us for three days, I loved her a lifetime's worth. I held Ella for her first and last breaths on this earth and I wrote these pages to chronicle her short, but momentous life. She accomplished a lot. She opened my eyes to life and brought the greatest joy in the world to my heart

I used to think about how people would talk about first steps, first words, etc. I always felt so robbed because I never got to experience these things. Although later I had other children to experience these things it was never the same as doing it with your first born child. I was so angry that I was denied these experiences; it wasn't until much later in life I was able to appreciate them.

My parents and I had many conversations about parenting and

children when I found out that I was going to be a parent. We never discussed how to handle this level of grief and what happens when your child dies before you.

I responded to this tragedy by trying to hyper control everything. I didn't realize until years later that you can't always do everything yourself. I have had many fears about putting this book into print because it does portray parts of me that I have struggled to keep private, but I realize now that the pain I have experience could perhaps help someone else as well as gather attention and support for the great organization The Compassionate Friends of Port Alberni.

Every year I celebrate her birthday by giving her three long stemmed red roses. One for each day of her life. I choose to focus on her birthday rather than the day she left me. There have been many books written on grief and loss and they all list different strategies and ways to deal with grief. I found this angering in many situations as they were written by people from an academic perspective rather an experiential one. They stressed the stages of grief and how long a person should be in one stage and how you had to do this at that stage, etc. I think that whatever you need to do is the right thing for you. Everyone is different and loss affects each person differently and people should not be told how they should feel. The only perspective I can add is that it is okay to ask for help. A friend of mine posted on his Facebook that anxiety and depression are not signs of weakness, but instead a sign that you have remained too strong for too long. This message resonated with me very strongly. I have always prided myself on being strong. What I realized in the intervening years was that my definition of strength was what was wrong. I should have been shooting for resilience. Although the main message with this book that I wanted to get out was that it is okay to ask for and more importantly receive help from people and not to stress a particular grief resource, I have included some in the back of this book that were extremely helpful for me and might be of some benefit for you. One of the negative consequences of not dealing with your emotions and conflicts and just stuffing them down is no matter how deep you stuff it, it always comes back, usually multiplied many times. I think our bodies have ways of telling us things when it is time to deal with stuff, some people have heart attacks which force them to re-evaluate things. My wakeup call was my appendix rupturing on June 5, 2004. I knew something was wrong. It happened at work and I stupidly finished my shift and then went out with co-workers. I eventually went to the hospital 12 hours later against my will and was rushed into emergency surgery. My stupidity didn't stop there, after checking myself out of the hospital the next day, to going back to work seven days later, my stubbornness knew no bounds. I told people it was no big deal, but I did know something was wrong and the plain truth is at that moment, I just didn't care. I chased one crisis after another including two car accidents. I went from one problem to another never taking the time to evaluate things and deal with them once and for all. It took years for me to gain some perspective on it all and realize how intimately connected our thoughts and emotions are to our health and well being.

I also wanted to honor Ella's memory because she is a part of my life and will always be. At first I wanted to hold onto the pain for as long as possible, because I was afraid I would forget her. Once you start talking about it, it hurts a lot, but the more you persevere and keep talking about it, it hurts a little bit less and less. The pain never goes away completely but it does metamorphisize from memories that are so painful that they take your breath away, to memories tinged with regret, and eventually joy. I also realized that by letting go of some of the pain you don't forget the person.

I choose to honor her and I am proud of what she was able accomplish in only three days of life. She revolutionized my life and taught me that life is not a spectator sport to be watched and withdrawn from but to participate in. Life should never be taken for granted. She taught me how much of a gift right now is. She opened my eyes to a different culture and brought many people together. As painful as the loss of her was, I am a better person for having known her. She made me more compassionate and understanding. I am very proud to have been her father.

Monday February 9, 2004

We went to my mom's house and burned the clothes that we held Ella with. We also burned food because I was told that we were supposed to offer something. The smoke rose up and touched us all and then went out. When we walked away I was told not to look back. There were many bizarre occurrences that happened. When a discussion of pallbearers came up my first thought was Wayne White and as soon I mentioned his name, the phone rang and it was Wayne.

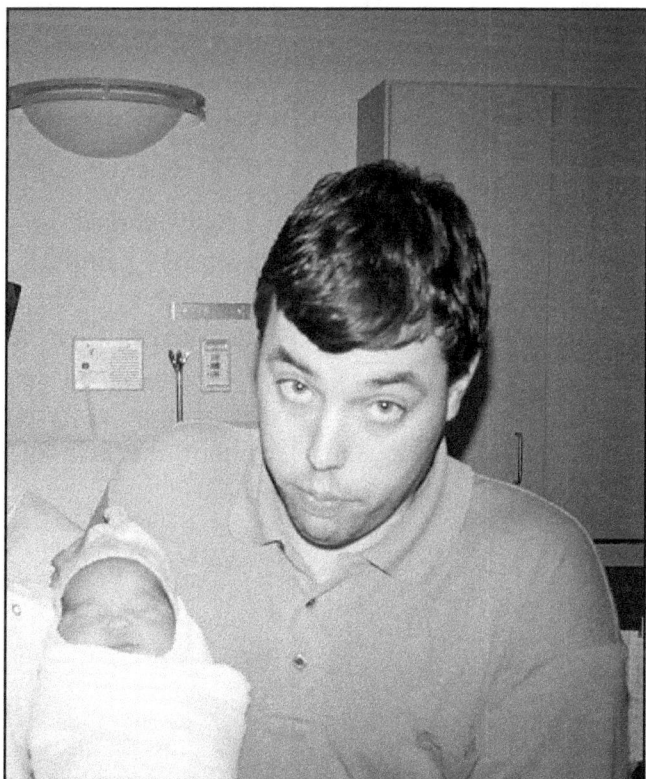

Me and Ella posing for yet another photo. I was tired of posing for photos but in retrospect very glad that people insisted on the photos.

Tuesday February 10, 2004

I spent the day getting photos produced. I went to Patty's Grandpa Archie's house and met with him and discussed what was going on. He told me how honored he was with the choice of Ella's name. My daughter was the first to wear the name in three generations. I gave him one of the two special photos and I kept the other one. Archie told me he would keep it covered for one year which was his tradition. The great people at Bella's Fabrics worked feverishly to create her dress. This was a last minute job which they created and did an incredible job of.

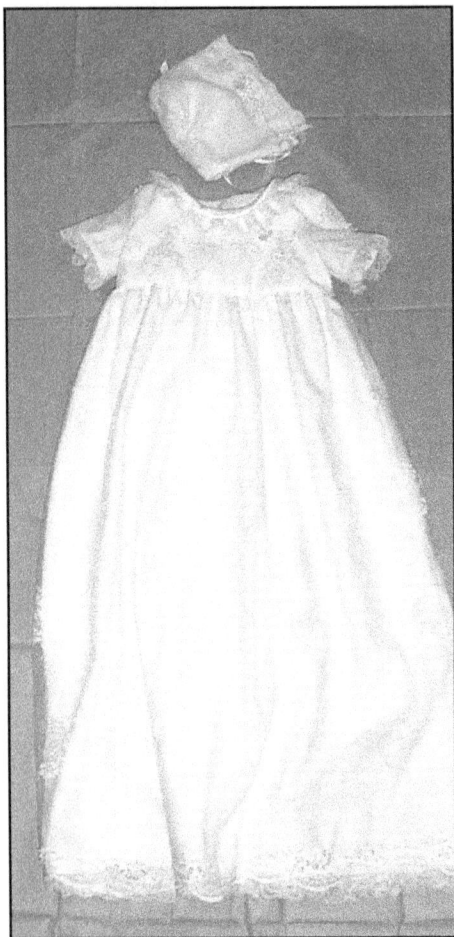

I also worked to get Ella's memorial pamphlet created and printed. There was so much to do that it seemed overwhelming. I could never have gotten everything done without the help of a lot of people.

Ella's dress was created by the incredible people at Bella's Fabrics.

Wednesday February 11, 2004

I went to the Notre Dame Church to choose the songs and readings that would be done at Ella's Service. We had a prayer service at the funeral home. I was against doing this at first as I didn't want other people to see her. It turned out to be the right decision to hold one and I am glad I was persuaded to. The funeral home did an excellent job. She looked like she was just about to wake up. There was a tiny tear in her left eye which made me upset. I was told that this was a good sign. I was told it was bad to cry over her and not to let any of my tears land on her. I was never told why that was. In the evening we took all of the baby stuff down and moved it to my mom's house where it was to sit for a year. Neither I nor Patty was allowed to touch the stuff. It had to be done by someone who was done having children. This was another cultural belief which I didn't know about. I had my hair cut and my hair was burned later as well. I believe now in the importance of having a viewing despite its difficulty. It helps with the closure and some of the essential healing, even if it doesn't feel like it at the time.

Thursday February 12, 2004

We held Ella's Service at the Notre Dame Church. It was a beautiful service. I have to admit I don't remember a lot of it. I remember trying to read something we had prepared and just being unable to read it. Wayne White and Jason Williams were Ella's pallbearers. As we left the funeral home they spun Ella counterclockwise four times which I was told was a tradition to start someone on their journey. She was also laid to rest facing east. There were several hundred people at the service to offer their support. At the gravesite the father blessed a crucifix and gave it to us and told us to keep it near us always. Archie said some words and a prayer in his language. I am not sure what was said.

Ella's service was a pretty good combination of both sides of her culture. We did do a traditional service at the Notre Dame Catholic Church. Prior to this we all went to the river to be cleansed as well as getting our hair cut. I had never known that the reason this is done is so that the spirit of the departing person will not recognize you and move onto their proper rest. I laid her to rest with my grandmother and grandfather, my mom's parents. I felt like this was the best option because Ella would be looked after.

We held a tea at the Hanson Hall which had an excellent turn out to honor Ella. Archie stressed at Hanson Hall that Ella should be remembered as a princess due to the blood that flows in her veins. There was a conflict between two of my friends. They were the best of friends and had not spoken for some time. This is something Ella did she brought them back together. That is a big job for a child. I hope that I can generate as much love, joy and compassion in others, the way Ella has done in me.

Friday February 13, 2004

I bought some blankets so Ella would be warm and some toys. I was told that if you burn them, she receives them on the other side. This was something I also did for Christmas and her birthday.

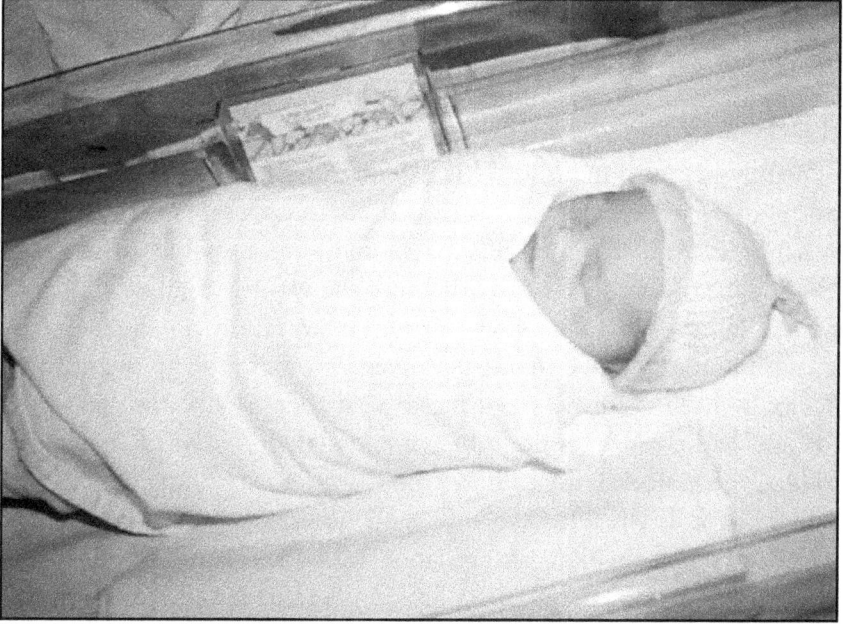

Ella resting after a busy morning of photos.

COMPASSIONATE FRIENDS

One of the aspects that Ella brought was the awareness of the Compassionate Friends Association of Port Alberni. Without my loss I would never have heard of this excellent organization and the great people and the incredible support they offer to people who are in pain. My dad also wrote several stories to let people know about this organization. I have included these stories here as well. They offer an insight into a grandparent's grief and how Ella affected him. They also show my dad trying to channel his pain into a constructive and hopefully helpful function. This is something I am trying to do with this book as well. My dad always told me to remember that everyone you meet is afraid of something, loves something, and has lost someone. Ella touched other lives as well because she was the catalyst for Ike to write about the Compassionate Friends Organization. I remember him asking me to his office to ask permission to write the story and then having written them he asked me to read them. He always respected me and had a lot of pride in his granddaughter. It was hard for me to read those stories due to how close I was to everything. It allowed me to see a different side of him and how he was hurting as well. Sometimes it feels like you are alone with your hurt and pain, like it's just you against the world. Sharing Ike's pain and seeing it from a different perspective allows you to open up with someone else. My dad was a huge supporter of the great work the Compassionate Friends Association does and I hope some of his articles and the feelings they conveyed made something easier for the people that read them. I know that they opened my eyes to the help they offer.

2007 by Ike Patterson

O kay, I'll admit it! I didn't really want to do this story, because frankly, it hurts to think about it, let alone write about it. But I know this article is too important to leave alone, because it can help a lot of people who are suffering from the loss of a child.

What do I know about the loss of a child? What qualifies me to write about perhaps the greatest loss in the world? I watched helplessly as my child suffered from the loss of his four day old child.

Sure I had experienced loss before, an older brother at the young age of seven. As I went through life, a sister and her children were taken, my mother, countless friends and acquaintances – But never the loss of my own child.

"You never said it would hurt so bad," my son said to me on that unforgettable day. "I didn't know" were the only words that I could manage as I cried with him. Hurting as I was over the loss of a beautiful granddaughter, I still couldn't say "I know how you feel," because I hadn't experienced his massive loss – the loss of his first child.

But there are people in the Valley who can say those words. Parents who have suffered the worst possible kind of heartache – the loss of a son or daughter. Colleen Deederly is one of those parents and one of the Compassionate Friends of Port Alberni.

"We're not counselors, we're just listeners," Colleen explained.

"We try to help you through the stages of grief. We call ourselves the group that nobody wants to belong to."

Colleen and her husband Ray, Sharon and Robert Mather, are a few of the hurting parents who ten years ago formed the local chapter of Compassionate Friends, which is part of a worldwide support organization for bereaved parents.

"Sharon and I felt that we needed a group to help us and somehow we talked to Kenn Whiteman who had done some searching and came up with this Compassionate Friends", Colleen recalled. "Sharon went to Vancouver

21

one day and connected with the BC Director for Friends. She came to Port Alberni and helped us get started – that was in November of 1997, ten months after Ray and I lost Jason."

The Christmas season is the most painful time of the year, when you've suffered the loss of a child and that's why each year, on the second Sunday in December, this year Dec. 9th, the Port Alberni Friends will hold their 'Candle Light Service' at the Echo Field House.

"Candles are lit at 7pm local time this Sunday," Colleen remarked.

"Hundreds of thousands of people light candles at the same time, around the globe, as the Compassionate Friends Worldwide service unites family and friends to honour and remember children who have died at any age from any cause."

Those who plan to attend this Sunday – and it's not only for parents, it's for siblings, grandparents as well as other family members and friends who want to support the parents – are asked to bring a candle, a picture of the child they have lost and to please arrive at the Echo Field House at least 15 minutes prior to the service starting.

"We can understand the pain," Colleen admitted. "Because we've had the loss. It's like living with a broken heart, but if we can help, please call me."

Colleen Deederly (sitting on the left), is joined by Sharon Mather on the right and standing (left to right) are: Robert Mather, Helga Fry and Al Fry. The plaque on the bench reads: "Dedicated to the memory of all our precious children, Compassionate Friends of Port Alberni."

2008 COMPASSIONATE FRIENDS PREPARE TO HONOUR MEMORIES OF THEIR CHILDREN
by Ike Patterson

*T*his is not your usual "night before Christmas" story, although it does happen at night and it is about sharing – the most pain parents can endure – the loss of a child.

This is the story of how some local hurting parents found a way to live with the deep sorrow that comes with such a loss. Eleven years ago, they formed the Port Alberni Chapter of the "Compassionate Friends", an international self-help organization for bereaved families who have experienced the death of a child at any age.

"We can understand the pain," Colleen Deederly, one of the founding parents offered. "Because we've had the loss. We try to help you through the stages of grief. We're not counselors, we're just listeners."

As you can imagine, the Christmas season can be extremely hard as families remember a child who is no longer with them. That's why each year, on the second Sunday in December, this year Dec. 14, the Port Alberni Friends hold a "Candle Lighting Service" at the Echo Field House.

"Candles are lit at 7pm," Colleen explained. "Hundreds of thousands of people light candles at the same time, around the globe, as the Compassionate Friends Worldwide Service unites family and friends to honour and remember children who have died at any age, from any cause."

For those who plan to attend this Sunday – and it's not only for bereaved parents, siblings, grandparents as well as other family members and friends who want to support the parents – are asked to please arrive at the Echo Field House at least 15 minutes prior to the service starting.

"Parents are asked to bring a stand-up picture of their child and a candle," Colleen advised. "We are also asking that parents please bring along a helium balloon because this year after the service, which is about 35 to 40 minutes long, we are going to have a balloon release. We will be attaching little glow lights to the balloons and releasing them from the Field House patio."

23

Colleen will have extra candles, the glow sticks and some balloons on hand this Sunday night. "Various kinds of helium balloons are available at Safeway," she added.

Anyone wanting more information about this Sunday's service at the Echo Field House is urged to call Colleen at 250-723-2365.

Remember, if you are a bereaved parent, YOU ARE NOT ALONE! You have friends – Compassionate Friends!

Judith Slobbe, Betty Argotow and Colleen Deederly are three of the Compassionate Friends of Port Alberni, who will be at this Sunday's annual "World Wide Candle Lighting Service" at the Echo Field House. The service starts promptly at 7pm, so please arrive a few minutes earlier. The balloon release will follow the service.

2009 FOR SOME THIS CHRISTMAS WILL HURT
by Ike Patterson

I magine not looking forward to Christmas because the pain is too great. There are people – parents – right here in the Valley, who struggle to get through the festive season each year because they are suffering with the greatest pain of all – the loss of a child.

Like me, you probably know some of these folks, but if you have never lost a child, you will never know the terrible feeling they live with everyday. You may not know parents who are suffering because a lot of them don't talk about their loss. Although I have never lost a child, one of my children has. I was there and I am still here for him. Even though it has been over 55 years since my older brother was killed suddenly, I still remember my mother losing a piece of her heart that night.

Those are two of the reasons I agreed to help a few years ago when asked by a grieving mother to create awareness for a group locally that understands the unbelievable hurt that comes with losing a child, at any age.

Colleen Deederly told me about forming the Port Alberni Chapter of "Compassionate Friends", an international self help organization for bereaved families, twelve years ago and how they continue to be available with support.

"We're not counselors, we're just listeners," Colleen offered. "We fully understand the pain because we've had the loss. We try to help you through the stages of grief."

Because the Christmas season can be extremely hard for families as they remember a child who is no longer with them, a special time is set aside each year on the second Sunday in December when the Port Alberni Friends hold a "Candle Lighting Service" at the Echo Field House.

"Candles are lit exactly at 7 pm," Colleen explained. "Hundreds of thousands of people light candles at the same time, around the globe, as the Compassionate Friends Worldwide Service unites family and friends to honour and remember children who have died at any age, from any cause."

For those who plan to attend this Sunday – and it's not only for bereaved parents, siblings, grandparents as well as other family members and friends who want to support the parents – are asked to please arrive at the Echo Field House at least 15 minutes prior to the service starting. "Parents are asked to bring a stand-up picture of their child and a candle," Colleen advised.

Some of the Compassionate Friends of Port Alberni gathered recently at the Harbour Quay to discuss this Sunday's annual World Wide Candlelight Service. Colleen Deederly, one of the founding members, (sitting on the left) was joined by Lorraine Payne on the right and standing (left to right) is Mark Payne, Helga Fry and Al Fry.

ELLA'S LEGACY

Vita Non Est Vivere sed valere vita est.

Life is more than merely staying alive

I began my journey of healing in earnest in 2011 when I was finally able to relinquish the baggage I was holding on to. It meant going through Ella's possessions including the moulds of her hands and feet given to me by Children's Hospital. I returned them to Ella's mother as a symbolic way of letting go of the emotional hostage they were holding over me. This was hard for me to let go of as they were the only physical things of her that I had. By letting go of these I realized I had carried them long enough and my journey was ready to take the next step. I know that it is not what we carry with us, but what we let go that defines us.

I learned a lot about first nation's culture through this experience. One of the parts we performed was an abbreviated naming ceremony. Ella would have the honor of being named. The name chosen was Katlah. I was told that this means the time of day between evening and the morning when the sun is just coming up. We also had her baptized as well as a chant was done the purpose of which was to announce and introduce her to ancestors, so that they would be there to greet her when she crossed over. I must admit I took a great comfort from this. I was already shattered by this time and I was grateful for this measure of respect for her. This was done when we knew how things were progressing. I will always have the utmost respect for Dr. Chessex and the team at Children's Hospital. They were incredible and although things didn't work out, it was not for a lack of effort on their part. I will always remember Dr. Chessex's kindness and candor. I needed to hear things as they were and not sugar coated and he gave it to me straight.

I have had many fears about putting this book into print because it does portray parts of me that I have struggled to keep private, but I realize now that the pain I have experience could perhaps help someone else as well as gather attention and support for the great organization The Compassionate Friends of Port Alberni.

Every year I celebrate her birthday by giving her three long stemmed red roses. One for each day of her life. She is always in my heart and will always be for the rest of my life until I get to see her again. I believe she is with my parents and they are looking after each other. I am sure of it. I bought a special ornament which I place on the tree every year.

Spirituality became much more important in my life. I participated in all souls night at the Catholic Church. It became important for me to honor people and become more grateful. It took me many years to come to this realization. I spent a lot of time being so angry at why me and what sin had I committed to be punished this way. I had always tried to live a good life and couldn't understand why this was happening. I was looking for a reason for all of what I was feeling. I realized later that there was no reason for it to happen. That is the worst part. There is not always a reason. For things to happen the way they do sometimes it is just a terrible thing and you have to accept that. That acceptance is so hard.

One of the things Ella taught me was connection. That every life has meaning and importance. I would not be the person I am today without the support of good people. I sometimes think that who you are and who you become depends on who you meet. I have had the great fortune to be surrounded by supportive and positive people. I was able to maintain some semblance of sanity during this time of my life due to the support of a lot of incredible people. I wanted to speak about those people and some

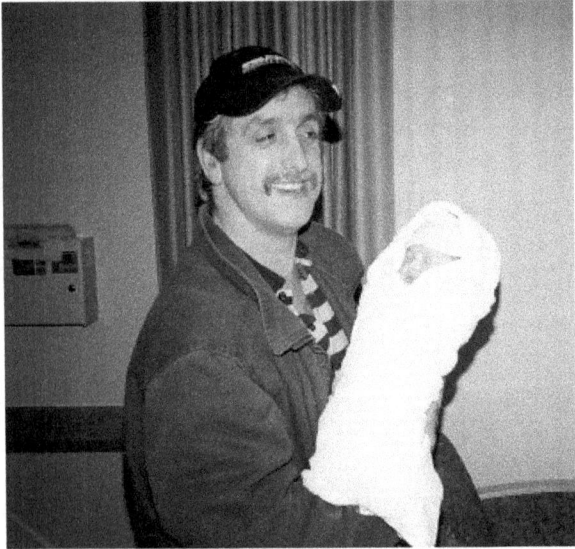

Wayne and Ella

of the support they gave me. My parents were incredible people who helped shape me and they were always there for me. Cheryl Lloyd's understanding and perspective allowed her to relate to me and enabled me to talk to her when I needed to and made me feel like whatever I was thinking or feeling was okay and I could talk to her whenever I needed to and that made me feel like there might be hope.

Wayne White for being there especially when it seemed like climbing inside a bottle was a good idea. A good friend should tell you what you need to hear, not just what you want to hear and in this regard Wayne is the best of friends. He snapped me out of a mindset when it could very easily have gone the other way. I will always be grateful for that.

Tanya Rasanen for making me laugh at a time in my life where there wasn't anything worth laughing about. Tanya also surprised me with a locket which has been a tangible source of strength for me. In 2009 I did the great lake walk from Youbou to Lake Cowichan. This is an annual event which people from all over come to participate in. I had set this as one of my challenges to see if I could do it after hearing about Shelley Harding's experience. I decided to accomplish some good by doing the walk as a fundraiser for Children's Hospital. I decided if I was walking for something rather than just myself it would give me extra motivation. The night before I left Tanya showed up at my house to present me with a locket. It contained Ella's photo and talked about people living on in your heart. This has become one of my most prized possessions. It definitely gave me strength during the walk and afterwards. I carried it daily with me for a long time. I began carrying it again during the writing of this book. It was the most heartfelt gift I had ever received. Tanya kept this as a secret from me. She had been planning it for some time. She later told me that giving it to me made her feel like she was on cloud nine and she literally floated home after giving it to me. I have included a photo of the locket here which has given me strength. The support Tanya gave me during the intervening years has helped me immeasurably with everything I was going through.

Norma Hennessey for being supportive. One of the only things I remember of Ella's funeral was a hug Norma gave me that was probably one of the best hugs I have ever received. It felt like for a moment, at that instant it gave me enough strength to go forward another step.

I shut down emotionally which I thought was the only way to deal with things. I next thought anger would be a better substitute. Holding onto anger is like grasping a hot coal with the intent of throwing it at someone else. You are the one getting burned.

The locket given to me by Tanya.

CONCLUSION

Istruggled with what to include in this book. It is difficult to judge what is too personal and should be left out. I really worried what people would think about me if they became of aware of some of the more unpleasant parts of my story. What I realized is that it shouldn't be censored because what made it so difficult is the story and it to me showcases how people can grow.

I carried a lot of guilt for a lot of years, thinking that maybe if I did something different or saw something maybe we could have got her help sooner. This is a destructive train of thought which will lead no where except more anger and pain.

I am certainly no expert or authority on grief, but I have experienced more than my fair share of loss. This perspective does give understanding to people and empathy for what they are going through. I wanted to write this book to let people know that is okay to feel the way they feel. I used to get so angry when people said you should do this, feel that or be in a certain stage of grief by a certain point of time. People heal differently in different ways and they are all what works for that individual person. I know that sometimes a person who can listen is the thing that people need the most. There are times when you don't want to talk about it or even can't. I know there are times when the pain is so deep and so a part of you that it seems like it will never go away. I also know that sometimes that can make someone think of extreme measures being the only remedy for the pain. I have been there. I do hope that if you ever need something I can help you with that. I have included resources in this book with some great people who can help. I have also included my contact info in the back. Please contact me if you need someone to listen.

I feel like I have a responsibility to help people whenever I can. I was always raised with a thought to the community and its people. I hope that my story will make someone feel like it is okay to let it out and that there are people out there who care and will listen, to whatever it is you need to say.

Sometimes grief affects people in different ways. When I went back to work it was hard because everyone was worried about what they said to you because they were afraid to hurt you and sometimes they would just say nothing at all. This was sometimes quite bad because it really multiplied the loneliness I was already feeling

I did keep some of Ella's belongings. One of things I kept was the hat that Ella wore at the hospital I sealed it in plastic and I would smell it occasionally. I never told people about it after people told me how weird it was. I have had many people come up to me since and tell me of their own individual rituals that they used to help cope with their loss

We all expect our parents to precede us in death. No one expects to have to make their child's funeral arrangements. And the loss of a child brings with it a special and persistent manifestation of grief that can feel "like a stomachache that never ends." Even though Ella was only with us for three days, I loved her a lifetime's worth. I held Ella for her first and last breaths on this earth and I wrote these pages to chronicle her short, but momentous life. She accomplished a lot. She opened my eyes to life and brought the greatest joy in the world to my heart.

Ella's short life has taught me to hang on to every moment and treasure it. From this day forward I will no longer ignore what is in my heart. I have always tried to keep a tight reign on my emotions and because of this and my fear I have lost out on several opportunities for happiness. I will no longer hesitate to express myself and spread as much joy and love as I can. Ella's passing has made me want to look into bettering myself and see if I can find some answers. As I write this my heart is neither full, nor empty. I have lost a part of myself which I can never replace, but I am happy for the three days I was given with my daughter. I cannot express the gift the greatest gift which Ella has given me. She has taken my anger from me. There are people I have hated truly detested and this anger was polluting my soul and robbing my life of all meaning and happiness. It is like Ella's love washed my soul clean and purified me. I promise you Ella that I will not waste the gifts you have given me and I love you very much baby. I promise I will never forget you and we will be together again one day.

AFTERWORD

To tell Ella's story was a monumental task for me to undertake. How much detail do I put in? How much is too personal? Do I want to upset people? These were some of the questions I dealt with. I also had to grapple with all of the emotions I had avoided and how I handled a lot of the hurt. I wanted to make something that would help other people and at the same time honor Ella and let her know that I was thinking of her. The method of telling has as much meaning and importance as the story itself. I have tried to keep the book as accessible as possible.

I suffered a great loss after Ella passed away. With her death I became trapped in despair so deep I thought I couldn't go on living. As I wrote this book, nothing was harder than returning to those memories. I know my decision to publish this book is the right one. The pain taught me what it meant to be alive. As you live you etch your life inside other people.

The Navajo have a saying that the spirit of the person lives as long as someone who lives remembers them. I will always remember you Ella.

ACKNOWLEDGEMENTS

There was a lot of work that went into this book from my end but no book is ever completed alone. First and foremost, I would like to thank Phil Littlewood for helping to create the finished product. I couldn't have done it without him. I also received a lot of support and encouragement from some of the people I work with.

I would like to specifically thank my co-worker Chris Finlayson and his wife Anthea. I was quite stuck with an image to use for the cover and had gone through several ideas, only to reject them all. I spent so much time fixated on the cover that I stopped writing. When I was venting, Chris mentioned a photo he had taken. The back cover image of this book was taken by his wife on Sunday September 2, 2012 at Chup Point of the Alberni Inlet. This photo turned out great and had a connection as it was taken at the time of day that Ella's name represents.

RESOURCES

"When the Bough Breaks: Forever After the Death of a Son or Daughter", by Judith R. Bernstein, a psychologist and a bereaved parent, whose twenty-six year old son, Steven, died of cancer. She does not talk about recovery since she doesn't believe in that concept. Instead she weaves her experience and the contributions of fifty other broken-hearted parents into a wonderful tapestry full of hope and resiliency. This book will help you understand that what you are feeling is normal, and you are not alone.

"The Bereaved Parent", by Harriett S. Schiff. This highly recommended book provides sensitive and practical advice and necessary information to those who have "stared at hell and survived". As a bereaved parent herself, Schiff's tender and compassionate treatment of this painful and sensitive subject makes her book a classic.

Forgive and be Free: Michael Wickett: I purchased this as an audio program and when I listened to it and applied the information that it contained, it was powerful in releasing a lot of the anger and grief I was holding onto as well as guilt. The exercises are simple but they are not easy. They are emotionally powerful but worth it in the end if you work through them.

Journaling has also been helpful for me. I never wanted to feel like a burden to people. I used to feel like it was my burden to carry alone. Music and nature have also had a healing part to me. I don't know how many hours I spent outside looking for answers. The vast majority of this book was written down by the water. The support of good people help as well.

Compassionate Friends Association: They have chapters everywhere including Port Alberni.

If you need someone to listen or talk to I can be reached at kpatterson@avtimes.net

www.ingramcontent.com/pod-product-compliance
Lightning Source LLC
Chambersburg PA
CBHW061757040426
42447CB00011B/2352